ROCKS, MINERALS, AND RESOURCES

Fossils
Clues to ancient life

Rona Arato

Crabtree Publishing Company
www.crabtreebooks.com

Crabtree Publishing Company
www.crabtreebooks.com

Coordinating editor: Ellen Rodger

Editor: Carrie Gleason

Production coordinator: Rosie Gowsell

Design: Samara Parent

Proofreader and Indexer: Adrianna Morganelli

Art director: Rob MacGregor

Photo research: Allison Napier

Consultant: Dr. Richard Cheel, Professor of Earth Sciences, Brock University

Photographs: AP/Wide World Photos: p. 6 (bottom), p. 20 (top); Tom Bean/CORBIS/MAGMA: p. 7 (bottom); Bettmann/ CORBIS/MAGMA: p. 19 (top); Biophoto Associates/ Photo Researchers, Inc: p. 10 (top); Jonathan Blair /CORBIS /MAGMA: p. 6 (top), p. 13 (top), p. 16 (top); De Agostini/ NHMPL: p. 17 (bottom); David R. Frazier /Photo Researchers, Inc.: p. 14 (bottom left); Rose Gowsell: p. 27 (top); Roger Harris/SCIENCE PHOTO LIBRARY: p. 14 (top); Eric and David Hosking /CORBIS /MAGMA: p. 12 (bottom left); Joyce Photographics /Photo Researchers, Inc.: p. 11 (middle right); Layne Kennedy /CORBIS /MAGMA: p. 22 (bottom); Ted Kinsman /Photo Researchers, Inc.: p. 21 (top); Mehau Kulyk /Photo Researchers, Inc.: p. 15 (bottom); David Liebman: p. 12 (top); Michael Long/NHMPL: p. 16 (bottom); Sally A. Morgan; Ecoscene/CORBIS/MAGMA: p. 12 (bottom right); Linda J. Moore: p. 19 (bottom); The Natural History Museum, London: p. 11 (top), p. 23 (bottom); Richard T. Nowitz/ Photo Researchers, Inc.: p. 22 (top); Kevin Schafer/CORBIS/ MAGMA: p. 1; Mark A. Schneider /Photo Researchers, Inc.: p. 11 (middle left); Peter Scoones /Photo Researchers, Inc.: p. 7 (top); Sinclair Stammers/SCIENCE PHOTO LIBRARY: p. 18 (top); Kim Steele/Getty: p. 14 (bottom right); Sheila Terry /Photo Researchers, Inc.: p. 17 (top); Dung Vo Trung /CORBIS /MAGMA: p. 21 (bottom); Vo Trung Dung/CORBIS SYGMA/MAGMA: p. 23 (top); Dr. Paul A. Zahl /Photo Researchers, Inc.: p. 13 (bottom)

Illustrations: Connie Gleason: p. 3; Dan Pressman: p. 10 (bottom), p. 11 (bottom); Jim Chimpyshenko: p. 8, p. 25; Rob MacGregor: p. 24; Roman Goforth: pp 4- 5, p. 9, p. 15 (top)

Cover: Fossils help us to learn about plant and animal species that lived long ago.

Title page: Animal skeletons are perfectly preserved in layers of rock.

Crabtree Publishing Company

www.crabtreebooks.com   1-800-387-7650

Cataloging-in-Publication Data

Arato, Rona.
   Fossils / written by Rona Arato.
      p. cm. -- (Rocks, minerals, and resources)
   Includes index.
   ISBN 0-7787-1419-5 (rlb) -- ISBN 0-7787-1451-9 (pbk)
   1. Fossils--Juvenile literature. 2. Paleontology--Juvenile literature.
I. Title. II. Series.
      QE714.5.A73 2005
      560--dc22
                                              2004012807
                                                   LC

**Published in
the United States**
PMB 16A
350 Fifth Ave.
Suite 3308
New York, NY
10118

**Published
in Canada**
616 Welland Ave.,
St. Catharines,
Ontario, Canada
L2M 5V6

**Published in the
United Kingdom**
73 Lime Walk
Headington
Oxford
0X3 7AD
United Kingdom

**Published
in Australia**
386 Mt. Alexander Rd.,
Ascot Vale (Melbourne)
V1C 3032

Contents

Trapped in tar

The young horse eyed the shimmering water. The scorching heat made his mouth feel as dry as the sun-baked earth beneath his hooves. As he leaned forward to drink, his legs slipped. He fell in and became stuck in the sticky asphalt beneath the water's surface. A passing saber-toothed tiger, attracted by the terrified horse's cries, jumped in after him, hoping to make the colt his dinner. The tiger, too, became ensnared in the thick, gluey tar.

The La Brea Tar Pits

Millions of years later, the gummy asphalt pools became known as the Rancho La Brea Tar Pits, one of the richest sources of ancient **mammal** fossils in the world. Included in the fossil finds were an armored hide from an **extinct** ground sloth, and the only complete skull of a saber-toothed tiger ever found.

Over one million fossils have been extracted from the La Brea Tar Pits. The animals were trapped during the last of four great **ice ages**, about 11,000 years ago. For several hundred thousand years, they had lived in the area that is now Los Angeles. Today, a museum for the fossils includes a laboratory where visitors can see how the fossils are handled. Pit 91 is a working excavation where **paleontologists** are still digging out fossils trapped in the tar.

Clues to ancient life

Fossils provide a record of life on Earth. Fossils reveal evidence of ancient life that is preserved in sediment or sedimentary rock. Fossils range from tiny plants and animals to the bones of enormous dinosaurs.

Why study fossils?

Scientists learn about past life on Earth and how the Earth has changed over millions of years from fossils. Fossils tell what animals and plants lived and died out at different times. By examining fossils and the rocks they are found in, scientists understand the effects that events such as mass extinctions, **meteorite** impacts, and climate change have on Earth's history. Fossils provide a valuable look into our past, but they do not tell the whole story. Many plants and animals did not become fossils.

Body fossils

Body fossils are the whole body or parts of the body of a plant or animal. To become a body fossil, some part of the **organism** must not decay or rot. Skin and **internal organs** rot, but bones do not. Plant material rots, so plants occur only as **imprint fossils**. Most body fossils are found buried in sediment, or layers of rock and soil. In rare cases, extreme cold freezes an organism, similar to the way a freezer preserves food. In very dry conditions, such as deserts, a dead animal loses its moisture and shrivels up.

(top left) Sometimes, the internal organs of an animal can be fossilized, as seen in this frog.

(right) This baby dinosaur lived about 113 million years ago. It is a body fossil.

Trace fossils

Trace fossils are markings left behind by an organism such as footprints, trails, burrows, and nests. Scientists learn about the movement and behavior of animals from trace fossils. Coprolites are fossilized animal waste. Paleontologists learn what an animal ate from its coprolite.

(below) Dinosaur footprints are trace fossils. The footprints give clues as to how fast the dinosaur moved, whether it stood on two or four legs, and if it traveled alone or in herds.

Coelacanth fish and ferns are called "living fossils." They have been around for millions of years.

Sea fossils

Over 2,000 years ago, Greek scientists found fossils of sea life in the Pindus Mountain range, in Greece. They said the fossils proved that the mountains had at one time been under the sea. Most people refused to believe them. Today, scientists know that oceans at one time covered most of the Earth then receded, leaving behind dry land. Life began in the sea and has existed about eight times longer than life on land. Many more sea animals than land animals have been preserved.

Earth's past

When Earth first formed about 4.6 billion years ago, it was a boiling hot sea of molten lava, or hot liquid rock. As it cooled, a thin crust formed on the surface. Water vapor, or water in its gas form, was pushed out of the Earth's interior. When the Earth's temperature dropped below 212° Fahrenheit (100° Celsius) the water vapor condensed **and formed clouds, which caused rain. Over thousands of years, the rain filled rivers, lakes, and oceans.**

Land forms

The oldest rocks yet to be found were formed more than four billion years ago. Mountains and volcanoes were created by the constant changing, wearing down, and reshaping of the Earth's crust through earthquakes and volcanic eruptions.

200 million years ago

Pangaea

About 200 million years ago, the continents were connected in one super continent called Pangaea. An enormous ocean called Panthalassa surrounded this landmass. Scientists believe that North America was much further south than it is today. Plate tectonics caused Pangaea to break apart. Plate tectonics is the **theory** that the Earth's outermost layer is divided into seven large rocky pieces, or plates. The slowly moving plates pull apart, sideswipe each other, or crash together. A giant space between what is now northern Africa and western Eurasia opened up and filled with seawater.

65 million years ago

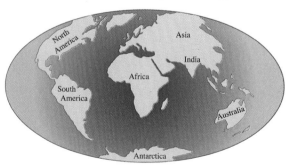

Today

Fossils of similar dinosaurs, mammals, and plants have been found on distant continents.

Early life

Scientists think the earliest life forms were simple **one-celled** organisms that developed over three billion years ago in the sea. Two billion years later, the organisms began forming into more **complex** life forms. Eventually, some crawled onto land. Around the same time, plant life began to appear.

The ice ages

Two million years ago, there began a series of ice ages in which all or parts of the Earth were covered in thick sheets of ice. These were followed by short, warm periods. The last ice age ended about 11,000 years ago, leaving behind the frozen ice caps of the North and South Poles. During the ice ages, animals that could not flee to warmer climates died out.

1. Precambrian Era: the first four billion years

Geologic time covers the physical formation and development of Earth. Scientists have divided the Earth's geologic history into four eras. Each era, except the Precambrian, is subdivided into periods.

2. Palaeozoic Era: from 570 to about 240 million years ago

- Cambrian
- Ordovician
- Silurian
- Devonian
- Carboniferous
- Permian

3. Mesozoic Era: from 240 to about 65 million years ago

- Triassic
- Jurassic
- Cretaceous

4. Cainozoic Era: from 65 million years ago to today

- Tertiary
- Quaternary

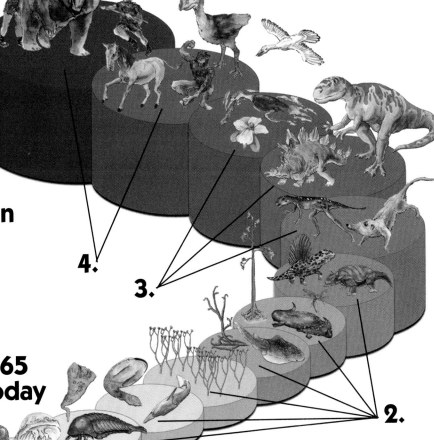

How fossils form

Earth's crust is made up of different types of rock. Fossils are found in rock. There are three forms of rock: igneous, sedimentary, and metamorphic. Rocks are made up of different kinds of minerals. Minerals are solid, non-living substances made of elements.

Sedimentary rock

Most fossils are found in sedimentary rock. The word sediment means "something that settles." Sedimentary rocks are a mixture of dust, sand, mud, shells, **corals**, and other materials that settle underwater or on land, and **compress** under pressure. Sedimentary rock forms in layers called strata, with the oldest layer under the newer layers. When a plant or animal dies, it is covered by layers of sediment and preserved as a fossil. Many sedimentary rocks are fossil-rich, while others contain no fossils.

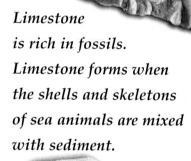

Limestone is rich in fossils. Limestone forms when the shells and skeletons of sea animals are mixed with sediment.

Making fossils

Few of the billions of organisms that have lived on Earth became fossils. For fossilization to occur, an organism must contain hard parts, such as a skeleton or shell. It has to be buried deeply right after it dies, before it decays from exposure to air, water, or **bacteria**.

The animal dies

is covered by sediment

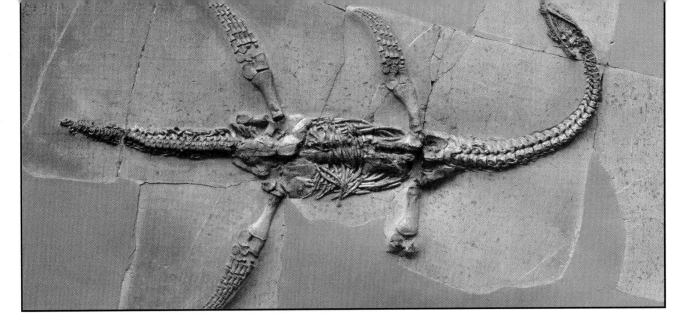

Igneous rock

Some igneous rocks form when magma rises to the surface through cracks or volcanoes, and cools. Other igneous rocks form when magma crystallizes within the Earth's crust. The word igneous means "fiery." Igneous rock does not contain fossils because the lava is so hot it burns any animals and plants it touches.

Granite is a type of igneous rock.

Metamorphic rock

Metamorphic rocks are rocks that are changed by heat and pressure. The word metamorphic means "change." Most metamorphic rocks are fossil-free because the pressures that changed them destroyed all evidence of fossils. Some rocks, such as slate, may contain traces of fossils, although their shapes are very different than when they were alive.

Slate is a type of metamorphic rock.

minerals replace body parts

is exposed at a later date

11

Types of fossils

Fossilization is the process through which an organism becomes a fossil. There are a variety of ways that fossils form. Some fossils contain the original organic **matter**. Other fossils are only imprints of the original plant or animal in rock.

Permineralization

One process through which a plant or animal becomes a fossil is permineralization. This happens when a plant or animal is quickly buried in sand or mud after it dies. Over time, the minerals that make up the bones and tissues of the animal are replaced by minerals that form rock, such as iron, silica, or calcite. Petrified wood is wood that has been turned to stone through permineralization.

Over time, mineralized water seeped into these ancient trees, replacing the wood fibers with a mineral called silica.

Compression

Compression is another way fossils form. During compression, a plant or an animal shell is covered by sediment. All that remains of the original organism is a thin layer of **carbon**.

Impressions

An impression is a mirror image of an organism in rock. Impression occurs when a plant or animal dies, leaving an image, or impression, of the way it looked. Impressions are commonly found in clay or silt.

(top right) A compressed sea scorpion from 250 million years ago.

(right) This 50 million-year-old fossil of an extinct fish is fossilized as an impression.

A mold of an ancient sea animal. The two pieces fit together to form an empty cast.

Molds and casts

Molds form when the hard parts of an animal, such as bones, shells, or teeth, are pressed into rock. A three-dimensional space is left after the animal decays. Sometimes, sediment fills the space, forming what is called a cast. Molds and casts do not contain any original organic matter. Scientists use molds to create replicas, or casts, of the animal.

Amber

Amber is fossilized resin, or sap, from ancient trees. Leaves or insects were sometimes trapped in the tree resin. The resin was buried and fossilized over millions of years, preserving the organism in perfect form. For thousands of years, people have prized amber's transparent gold, orange, green, or golden-brown beauty as a gem to be worn, traded, and used in decoration.

Burgess Shale fossils

The Burgess Shale is a fossil site in the Rocky Mountains in British Columbia, Canada. Over 500 million years ago, the continent of North America was closer to the equator. The sea animals that were fossilized in the Burgess Shale lived in warm shallow waters near a reef. Underwater mudslides killed the animals and quickly buried them in mud and clay at the base of the reef. Here, they were protected from air, bacteria, and **predators**. Over millions of years, sediment built up on top of the animals and turned them into fossils. The fossils from the Burgess Shale are unique because many of the soft body parts, such as gills, were also preserved.

A grasshopper trapped in amber 40 million years ago.

Dinosaurs

Dinosaurs are the most exciting of all fossil finds. Dinosaur fossils have been found on every continent in the world. Over 300 species of dinosaurs have been found and identified. By studying dinosaur fossils, scientists learn what these creatures were, where and when they lived, and why they became extinct.

Dinosaur evolution

Dinosaurs **evolved** from early reptiles over 230 million years ago during the Triassic Period. Reptiles are cold-blooded animals with scaly, waterproof skin. The earliest dinosaurs were only about ten to fifteen feet (three to five meters) long. They were bipedal, or walked on two legs, which leads scientists to believe that they moved very fast. During the Jurassic and Cretaceous periods, dinosaurs continued to evolve, becoming bigger and stronger than earlier species. During the Cretaceous Period, Tyrannosaurus Rex was one of the largest carnivores, or meat-eating dinosaurs. During the Jurassic Period, mammals began to develop.

(above)
Tyrannosaurus Rex may have been one of the most vicious of all carnivorous dinosaurs.

(above, right)
Compsognathus was the smallest dinosaur. It was the size of a chicken!

(left) The teeth of Tyrannosaurus Rex were as long as thirteen inches (33 cm).

There were two distinct types of dinosaurs. Some were reptilian, and others were bird-like. Dinosaurs are long gone, but birds, their closest living relatives, are living all over the world.

Dinosaur skin

Scientists do not know for certain what color dinosaurs were because there is no way to tell skin color from a fossil or an imprint. Some scientists think dinosaur skin was similar to that of modern crocodiles or alligators. Others think dinosaurs may have been many different colors, like modern lizards, with green, red, or brightly colored striped skin.

Disappearing dinosaurs

Scientists have many theories about what led to the extinction of dinosaurs. Dinosaurs, and 70 percent of all animal species, became extinct about 65 million years ago. Scientists think that a giant meteorite may have crashed into Earth and triggered the extinction. Another theory is that dinosaurs may have died out during one of the last ice ages. It is fortunate that we have fossilized remains that record the story of early life on Earth.

Paleontology

Paleontologists are scientists who study fossils to learn the history of life on Earth. Many paleontologists work at colleges and universities where they teach, conduct research, and write about the Earth's history. Others work for museums, searching for fossils and organizing exhibits.

Before the 1800s, people did not understand the history of life on Earth. Fossils had been found in rocks, but people did not know these were animals that had lived millions of years ago. Most people believed that all the plants and animals on Earth had always existed exactly as they were and that nothing ever changed.

Cuvier

In the late 1700s, Georges Cuvier, a professor at the National Museum of Natural History in Paris, France, reconstructed images of whole animals from a few bone fragments. When examining fossil bones, he described a flying reptile and a rhinoceros-sized sloth. Those were animals no one had ever seen. He named these pterodactyl and megathere and said they were from species that had died out. By identifying these new species, Cuvier founded the science of paleontology, the study of ancient life.

(above right) Pterodactyls were flying dinosaurs that lived about 200 million years ago.

(left) This illustration is based on the fossilized remains of a megathere.

In 1849, British scientist Richard Owen created the name dinosaur. Dinosaur comes from the Greek words meaning "terrible lizard."

Studying bones

Even before Cuvier, people had tried to identify fossil finds. In 1663, a German scientist put together fossils from several different species to make what he wrongly identified as a unicorn. Two years later, a book called *Micrographia* showed views of fossils and other natural objects as seen through the newly invented **microscope**. By the mid 1800s, scientists were looking for fossils all over the world. As fossil hunting became more common, the finds were displayed in museums. In 1922, the American Museum of Natural History began its own series of excavations in central Mongolia, China. They were looking for the remains of humans, but found dinosaur fossils instead.

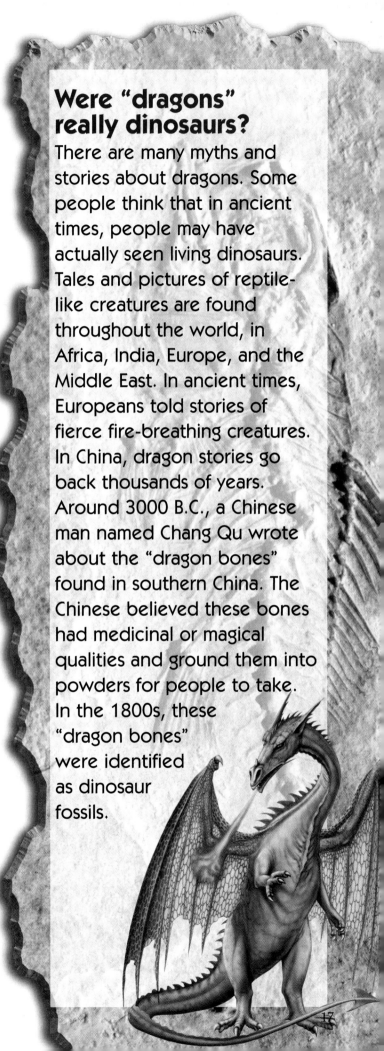

Were "dragons" really dinosaurs?

There are many myths and stories about dragons. Some people think that in ancient times, people may have actually seen living dinosaurs. Tales and pictures of reptile-like creatures are found throughout the world, in Africa, India, Europe, and the Middle East. In ancient times, Europeans told stories of fierce fire-breathing creatures. In China, dragon stories go back thousands of years. Around 3000 B.C., a Chinese man named Chang Qu wrote about the "dragon bones" found in southern China. The Chinese believed these bones had medicinal or magical qualities and ground them into powders for people to take. In the 1800s, these "dragon bones" were identified as dinosaur fossils.

Famous finds

Paleontologists are continually looking for new clues to the fossil puzzle. Their searches take them around the world, from major cities such as Los Angeles and Denver to distant places such as Patagonia in South America. Each discovery adds valuable information to our knowledge of Earth's history.

The search for baby dinosaurs

When paleontologist John Horner went to Montana seeking baby dinosaur bones, he had no idea of the historic find he would unearth. On a scrubby pasture on a Montana cattle ranch, he found a stony mound littered with tiny gray-black fossils. Gathering the scraps together, he assembled them into two complete infant duckbilled dinosaurs. There were many more bones, so he continued digging, eventually reaching a layer of red mudstone where the fossils stopped. Looking into the excavation, he saw that he had dug a bowl about six feet (two meters) across and three feet (one meter) deep. He had just discovered the world's first known dinosaur nest. Horner and his partner Bob Makela discovered seven more nests and identified two new species of dinosaurs. Horner also learned many new facts about how dinosaurs lived and acted. He had not only found the first dinosaur nests in North America, he had found the first dinosaur **nesting colony**.

Paleontologist John Horner holds a cast of a fossilized baby dinosaur beside a nest of dinosaur eggs.

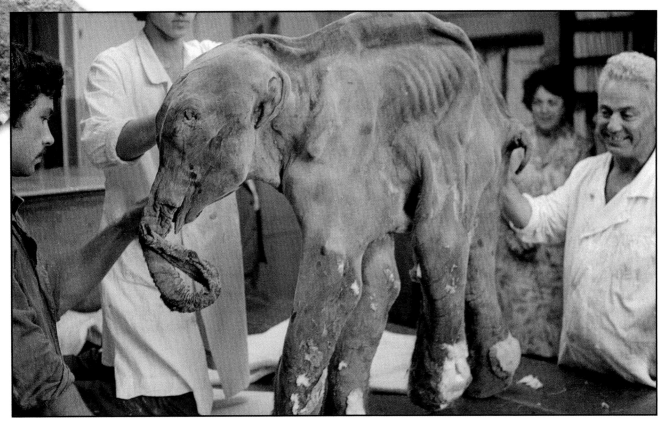

Dinosaur egg hunt

In the scorching hot desert of Northern Patagonia, in Argentina, scientists Luis M. Chiappe and Lowell Dingus found some dark gray rock fragments, crusted with small bumps and dents. The "rocks" were really dinosaur eggs. They had discovered the site of thousands of unhatched eggs that contained whole fossilized embryos that were over 65 million years old!

(top) In Siberia, this entire fossil of a baby mammoth was preserved in the ice for more than 10,000 years.

(right) An embryo is the name given to an animal while it is still developing, before it is born.

Woolly mammoth frozen in ice

One of the most famous finds occurred in Russian Siberia where paleontologists found a whole woolly mammoth, an elephant-like creature that lived 1.8 million to 11,000 years ago. The mammoth was found frozen in the ice. Woolly mammoths were one of the largest land mammals.

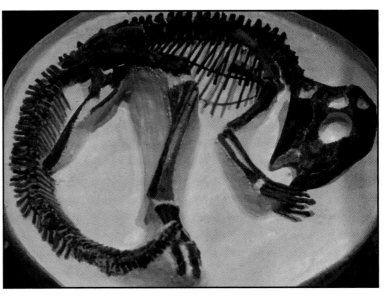

Finding fossils

Fossils are most common in dry areas with little vegetation and lots of bare rock. Many of the rocks that fossils are found in are ancient marine sediment that were once underwater. When the oceans receded, they left behind fossil-rich rocks.

The best places to look for fossils are in rocky **outcrops**, streambeds, and sea cliffs. Before collecting fossils, paleontologists must get permission from landowners to search for fossils and remove any they find. Paleontologists revisit the sites of past discoveries because rocks that were good sources once, may still hold valuable specimens.

Exposed fossils

Fossils are exposed during erosion or uplifting of rock. Erosion occurs when water runs over land, washing away surface rock and creating gashes in the earth. Uplifting happens when two plates of land under the Earth's surface crash into each other forcing one plate up and the other down.

(above) Paleontologists uncover a five million-year-old whale fossil in California.

(below) The Grand Canyon was formed by the Colorado River eroding the soil and rock. Many fossils have been found in the Grand Canyon's rocky outcroppings.

Paleontologists use special tools to dig for fossils. They are very careful not to chip or break off pieces of the fossils.

Dating fossils

After paleontologists find fossils, they figure out how old they are. One method of dating fossils is to use stratigraphy. Stratigraphy is determining how old a fossil is by how deeply it is buried in rock strata, or layers. Radiometric dating is a method of determining the age of rocks. Certain elements within rocks decay at different rates. When scientists test the elements, they determine the age of the rock and the fossil it contains. Scientists also compare the fossil with fossils from known periods found in the same location to determine its age.

Starting a fossil collection

Fossils are all around us. Most fossils are buried in sedimentary rock, so look for layers of soft rock, such as sandstone or limestone. Find out where sedimentary rocks exist in your area. If you look for fossils on private property, remember that you must ask permission. There are many places where fossil hunting is allowed. Check with the parks department in your area to find out where you can look. Once you have found a fossil, your detective work begins.

1. Keep a notebook. Write down where you found your fossil and what type of rock it was in.
2. Use a fossil guide to identify your specimen.
3. Bring your fossil to school and share it with your class. If you find something special, tell someone.

On site

Excavating, identifying, and preserving fossils takes a great deal of knowledge, skill, and teamwork. A typical team includes a paleontologist who studies the age of the fossils; a geologist who dates the rocks and the fossils found in them; a draftsperson who draws pictures of the fossils and workers who dig the bones out of the rocks; a photographer who takes pictures of the fossil finds, and technicians who prepare fossils for museum exhibits.

Excavation

Excavating, or digging fossils out of rock, is a slow and careful process. The rock is chipped away with picks and shovels. Most fossils are surrounded by material called **matrix**, that is carefully removed.

Once a bone is uncovered, it is brushed with **shellac** or quick-setting glue, so it does not crumble. Specimens are numbered so they can be reconstructed later at the lab. Large skeletons are cut apart to be moved. A draftsperson draws each bone in the exact position it was found. The photographer takes a picture of the site. Large bones are left half-buried in rock, and then cleaned in the lab. All fossils, large or small, are handled very carefully. Small fossils are packed in boxes or bags. Larger specimens are first wrapped in paper or burlap, and then packed in straw.

(above) The matrix is removed with small hand tools, such as dental picks.

(below) A paleontologist uses a jackhammer to clear soil at a dig site.

At a lab, technicians brush off the fossilized bones of a Titanosaurus. The bones were covered in plaster to protect them on the journey from the site to the lab.

Prep work

Cleaning a fossil is known as "preparation," or prep work. The lab where this is done is called the prep lab and the workers are called paleo-prep technicians. These scientists understand that each fossil is unique and, if broken, cannot be replaced. They use dental picks and small power hand tools, such as a mini jackhammer and a small sandblaster to carefully remove the rock surrounding the fossil. In some cases, they use an organic acid, such as vinegar, to take off hard rock that cannot otherwise be removed.

Assembling a skeleton

If the paleontologists have enough bones, they put together a skeleton of the animal. The first step is to make a steel frame to support the bones. The bones are then wired together, one by one. Missing bones are replaced with plastic or fiberglass copies. Dinosaur skeletons appear in museums around the world and show us what life on Earth was like millions of years ago.

Dinosaur bones on display at The Natural History Museum in London, England. Often, schools organize trips to museums so children can see the dinosaur bones close up.

Fossil fuels

Fossil fuels are the remains of once living organisms. Unlike fossils, these organisms have decayed and no longer retain their physical shape. Coal is a fossil fuel composed of ancient plants. Oil and natural gas are formed from the remains of animals. Fossil fuels are extracted from the ground and burned for energy.

Oil and gas

Oil and gas form when fossils are buried and are under extreme pressure over millions of years. A layer of **non-porous** rock covers the **reservoirs** and prevents the oil and gas from coming to the Earth's surface. To extract oil and gas, people drill through the reservoirs.

Coal

The Carboniferous Period, or Coal Age, was about 350 million years ago. It was a time of swamps filled with trees and plants, and lakes and oceans teeming with life. As living organisms died and decayed, the carbon in their bodies stayed behind. Over time, as layers of sediment covered the decaying plant and animal matter, the sediment's weight and pressure hardened it into carbon-rich coal.

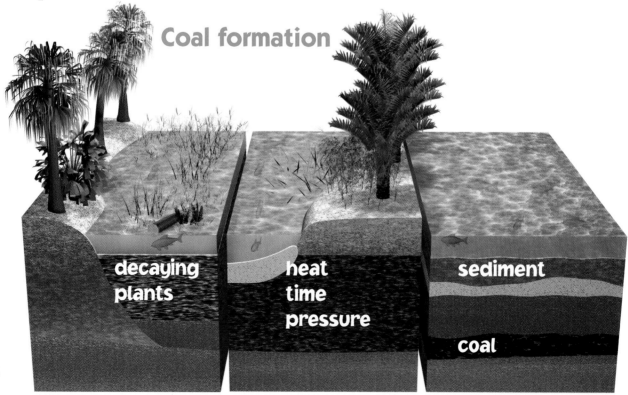

Coal formation

decaying plants

heat time pressure

sediment

coal

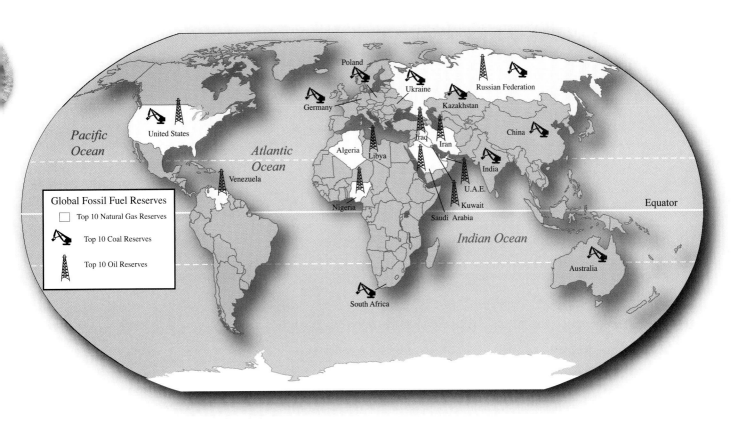

Global Fossil Fuel Reserves
- ☐ Top 10 Natural Gas Reserves
- Top 10 Coal Reserves
- Top 10 Oil Reserves

Map labels: Poland, Germany, Ukraine, Russian Federation, Kazakhstan, China, Iraq, Iran, Algeria, Libya, India, U.A.E., Kuwait, Saudi Arabia, Nigeria, United States, Venezuela, Australia, South Africa

Pacific Ocean, Atlantic Ocean, Indian Ocean, Equator

Where is oil drilled?

Oil, also called petroleum or crude oil, is used to run automobiles, planes, and ships, operate factories, and heat homes. Natural gas is often found underground in combination with oil. The world's major oil and natural gas fields are in the Middle East, in countries such as Saudi Arabia, Iraq, the United Arab Emirates, Kuwait, and Iran. In the United States, oil is found in several states, such as Alaska, California, Texas, and Oklahoma. There are also large oil fields beneath the ocean floors. Extracting oil from under the ocean is called offshore drilling. Most offshore drilling occurs in the North Sea, the Arabian Gulf, and the Gulf of Mexico.

Tar sands

While most oil is found underground, some is found mixed with loose sand on the Earth's surface. This type of oil deposit is called oil sands or tar sands. The biggest source of oil sands is in the province of Alberta in western Canada. Scientists believe the tar sands were formed when oil from southern Alberta was pushed northeast by the movement of tectonic plates. Water and bacteria eventually changed the crude oil into a heavy, sticky oil.

(above) This map shows where the major deposits of oil, gas, and coal are found worldwide.

Uses of fossil fuels

People's understanding of fossils as clues to the past is recent compared to how long they have been using fossil fuels. To kill their enemies in battle, ancient Persians and Greeks coated arrows with oil and set them on fire. The ancient Chinese burned oil for cooking and to light and heat their homes. Native Americans used oil to waterproof their canoes and kayaks.

Coal

Coal is one of the first fuels ever used. There is evidence that people burned it over 6,000 years ago to heat ovens for baking bread and firing pottery. It is an inexpensive and reliable fuel that is today burned for generating electricity, heating homes, and cooking. Around the world, 40 percent of all electricity is generated by coal. Coal is also used to make steel because steel plants need very hot fires that coal can produce.

Oil

Since ancient times, people have used oil to light their homes and workplaces. In addition to fuel and heating, oil is used in many of the products we use every day. In many parts of the world, natural gas and oil have replaced coal as fuel because they are cleaner to burn. They are used for heating homes and factories, cooking, running machinery and vehicles such as cars, airplanes, ships, and trains.

In a distillation tower at an oil refinery, crude oil is separated into gasoline, diesel fuel, grease, and other petroleum products.

Plastic

Plastic is made from oil. Plastic is used in everyday products such as radios, telephones, compact discs, cars, medical equipment, dishes, and toys. Nylon backpacks, polyester shorts, pants, and other clothing are all made from petrochemicals that start as oil.

The fuel for jet planes comes from fossil fuels.

A disappearing resource

As more people around the world drive cars, use electricity, and manufacture goods, the demand for fossil fuels increases. Fossil fuels are being used up faster than they are created. Scientists warn that we may run out of these **resources**. They are constantly working to develop other energy sources such as solar power, or energy from the sun. It is important that people conserve energy whenever possible. Turning off lights in empty rooms, walking or riding a bicycle short distances, and recycling glass, plastic, and other products are ways to conserve fossil fuels.

Wind power is an alternative to burning fossil fuels.

Pollution

Fossil fuels create harmful waste gases **when they burn. These gases pollute the environment, often turning the air brown, and cause health problems for plants, animals, and people.**

Smog

The word smog is a mixture of the words "smoke" and "fog." When fossil fuels such as coal or oil burn, the leftover **particles** mix with moisture in the air creating a brown haze that burns people's eyes, and causes headaches and breathing problems. Smog is mainly caused by emissions from cars and trucks and from factory smokestacks.

(above) Smoke stacks from a coal burning plant pollute the air around these homes.

Mexico City is one of the most polluted cities in the world. The haze over the city is caused by pollution from vehicles and factories.

Acid rain

Acid rain forms when waste gases mix with moisture in the air. This moisture rises up into clouds, and is released in rainwater that is acidic, or poisonous. Acid rain kills fish and poisons lakes. Many lakes in Canada and Scandinavia have been declared "dead lakes" because everything that once lived in them has been killed or poisoned by pollution. Acid rain damages buildings and statues made of limestone.

The greenhouse effect

A greenhouse is an enclosed environment built to grow plants. Our Earth is similar to a giant greenhouse. The sun's energy heats the atmosphere, or layers of gases surrounding the Earth and mixes with a gas called carbon dioxide. Without this heat, nothing on earth could live. Carbon dioxide is a gas released by burning fossil fuels. When automobiles and factories release too much carbon dioxide, the atmosphere overheats. Scientists call this the greenhouse effect or global warming. Too much warming may melt the polar ice caps, raising the level of seawater and causing massive floods along shorelines and in coastal cities.

Oil spills

Oil is transported in giant tankers or through pipelines that snake under oceans and across the land. When these are damaged, oil spills occur, polluting the land and water. The oil coats the skin of marine animals such as seabirds, seals, and fish, killing many of them.

(top) When oil spills into the ocean, the feathers of seabirds become coated with oil. The birds cannot fly or stay warm when covered in oil.

Survival

Throughout Earth's history, thousands of plant and animal species have appeared, evolved, and died out. The theory of evolution is only about 200 years old. Before that time, people believed that a divine force created each species exactly the way we see it today. As scientific discoveries unfolded, some people began to question the history of life on the planet.

Extinction

Scientists believe there have been many mass extinctions in Earth's history that determined which animals disappeared and which survived. The most recent was the Cretaceous-Tertiary extinction about 65 million years ago. Some scientists believe it was caused by a giant meteorite crashing into Earth. The crash may have triggered earthquakes, tidal waves, and forest fires that covered the planet with smoke and dust. Those are catastrophes that may have killed the dinosaurs.

Evolution

Evolution is the theory that species change by **adapting** to suit environmental conditions. Evolution means that life developed slowly and that every species on Earth comes from a common ancestor. The original one-celled organisms led to the trees, birds, flowers, fish, mammals, and humans on Earth today. We are all part of a huge family dating back to the beginning of life on Earth.

Family trees

Scientists study common characteristics among plant and animal families. These characteristics are carried in genes, the part of a living organism that contains the species' natural traits. It is because of genes that a child has the same color eyes as its mother or father. These characteristics are charted on a "family tree" called a phylogeny. Over thousands and millions of years, as new traits develop, or evolve, family trees sprout "branches" that become new, but related, species.

(below) The evolution of people from apes is an example of one species evolving from another.

Sharks - winners in the selection competition

The process whereby a species dies out or survives is called natural selection. Some species adapt to climate or other changes while others become extinct. Of all the animals that have lived on Earth, few have been around, almost unchanged, as long as sharks. Sharks appeared 430 million years ago, in the Silurian Period known as the "Age of Fishes." They most likely survived because of their sleek, streamlined bodies that help them swim without using much energy. Saving energy is important. Sharks never sleep and they never stop swimming!

Glossary

adapting Changing to suit the environment

asphalt A thick, sticky petroleum tar

bacteria Tiny one-celled organisms

carbon A chemical element found in all living things

complex Something complicated or intricate

compress To squeeze or press something together

condensed Changed from a gas to a liquid form

corals The hard skeletons of some marine animals

elements Basic substances that cannot be broken down

evolved Developed gradually into something else

extinct No longer in existence

ice ages Extreme cold periods when most parts of the world were covered in huge ice sheets called glaciers

imprint fossils The hollow imprint in rock of the remains of an animal or plant

internal organs Soft parts inside the body that have a specific function, such as the heart

mammal A warm-blooded animal that gives birth to fully developed, live young

matrix The solid matter in which a fossil is contained

meteorite A giant ball of rock and metal that travels through space

microscope A scientific instrument that magnifies, or enlarges, small things for viewing

nesting colony An area where groups of the same type of animal come together to build nests

non-porous Not having holes

one-celled A simple organism with only one type of body cell

organism A living being

outcrop Portions of bedrock, or the bottom layer of soil, that sticks out of the ground

paleontologists Scientists that study ancient life on Earth

particle The smallest bit of something

predator An animal that eats other animals

reservoirs Layers of sedimentary rock that have trapped oil and natural gas

resources Things that can be used

shellac A hard, protective finish

theory An idea or belief

waste gases Harmful gases created by burning fossil fuels

Index